This Journal b

_____

_____

_____

_____

Remember:

You are stronger than you think,

and the future holds good things for you.

BRENDON BURCHARD

HIGH PERFORMANCE
JOURNAL

BRENDON BURCHARD

HAY HOUSE, INC.

Carlsbad, California • New York City

London • Sydney • New Delhi

From the Desk of Brendon Burchard

To unlock the secret to lifelong happiness, success, connection, and fulfillment, begin with a deep commitment to personal development. We can't become who we are destined to be without self-awareness and self-mastery. We can't love and lead others with full heart unless we first understand ourselves. And we can't achieve a meaningful life without reflection and intention. If you agree, you're going to love this journal!

It's not one of those journals where you just stare at a blank page, wondering what to write about. It is a guided tour through advanced personal development that will help you forge the mindset, beliefs, and habits that will make you extraordinary! It's based on the science of high performance, which is a particular way of thinking about success, well-being, and relationships.

The best way to use this journal is to simply *use it every single day*. Growth comes from consistency in self-reflection, intention setting, taking action, and capturing and integrating our learning. This journal will help you do just that—so fill it out daily, please!

You've wanted more clarity, motivation, focus, and growth—this is the tool you've been waiting for!

In the pages ahead, you'll find three types of journal pages:

- On the left-hand pages, you'll find what I call a "high-performance prompt." Basically, I start a sentence for you, and you finish it. Then, in case you need more ideas or get stuck, I give you further questions to reflect upon at the bottom of the page.

- On the right-hand pages, you'll find a daily diary area—it's the same every day so that you can journal about your day's experiences, thoughts, circumstances, dreams, ideas, and musings, and develop a habit of self-reflection.

- Every few pages you'll find some of my most popular motivational quotes or musings. Feel free to take a photo of them and share on social media, or just scribble your own thoughts all around them. It's your journal—do what feels good! If you share on social media, please tag me @BrendonBurchard and use #GrowthDay. (GrowthDay is the name of our company! It's our belief that every day is a great day to grow. And when you journal and push yourself to think more deeply about your life, you do indeed grow every day!)

I'm so excited that you picked up this journal. I know the change it can make in your life. I've spent the past 20 years helping people transform their lives and achieve their dreams more quickly than they thought possible. I know the prompts ahead can make a real difference in how you think, feel, behave, and lead.

If you'd like more insights on these topics, be sure to order my book *High Performance Habits: How Extraordinary People Become That Way*. If you're a detailed planner and productivity freak like me, please also grab a copy of the *High Performance Planner* so that you can schedule your day, stick to your priorities, and score your habits every day, week, and month. Also, be sure to tune in to my podcast, *The Brendon Show*.

Please use this journal every day—don't leave your growth to randomness! Do the work. Explore. Learn. Write. Think. Plan. Dream. Return to these pages every day and you'll find yourself more open, focused, optimistic, and ready to take on the world! I'm so excited for you!

In everything you do, my friend, please remember: The future holds good things for you, and you are stronger than you think.

Your coach,
Brendon

P.S. When you've filled out your journal, or you want some for your family and friends, you can always order more at **GrowthDay.com/store**. (NEW: We have an app coming soon! So be sure to get on our mailing list so that we can get you the link!)

Our first prompt begins with gratitude,
of course. Gratitude is the golden frame
through which see the meaning of life.
So turn the page and begin to see life anew.

The 5 most important events that happened in my life that I am profoundly grateful for include . . .

[What happened in each event—who were you then, what did you see, feel, and experience? What do you remember most? Why are you grateful for each event specifically? What did you learn from the events? What lessons did you learn that you are applying (or could apply) to your current life?]

What's happening in your life today? What are you thinking about, feeling, or experiencing? How are your health, career, relationships, and mood? What were your intentions for today? What received most of your focus? What decisions did you make? How are things turning out? What emotions came up for you today? What habits made your day better? What strengths did you exhibit today? What tasks or goals did you achieve that you feel good about? What did you learn about someone today? What is something you appreciated today, or are appreciating at this stage of your life? Just start writing now. Don't worry about being perfect—just write what comes to mind every day!

If I could describe my ideal future in 2-4 paragraphs, this is how I would describe it . . .

[Describe any time period in your future—3, 5, 10, or 20 years from now. What are you like then? What are your greatest strengths? What brings you joy? Who and what is in your life that you feel so grateful for? What have you achieved? Who have you become? What's most meaningful to you? What are your days like? What are your values? What makes you most excited about your future?]

What's happening in your life today? What are you thinking about, feeling, or experiencing? How are your health, career, relationships, and mood? What were your intentions for today? What received most of your focus? What decisions did you make? How are things turning out? What emotions came up for you today? What habits made your day better? What strengths did you exhibit today? What tasks or goals did you achieve that you feel good about? What did you learn about someone today? What is something you appreciated today, or are appreciating at this stage of your life? Just start writing now. Don't worry about being perfect—just write what comes to mind every day!

If I could describe the kind of person I want to be in 3 words, those words would be . . .

[Write down as many words as you want, and then prioritize the ones that you think you most want to live into. Why are each of those words most important to you now? Have you been embodying those words recently? How can you demonstrate those words through how you show up and how you treat others? How can you remind yourself of those words, so you consistently live them?]

What's happening in your life today? What are you thinking about, feeling, or experiencing? How are your health, career, relationships, and mood? What were your intentions for today? What received most of your focus? What decisions did you make? How are things turning out? What emotions came up for you today? What habits made your day better? What strengths did you exhibit today? What tasks or goals did you achieve that you feel good about? What did you learn about someone today? What is something you appreciated today, or are appreciating at this stage of your life? Just start writing now. Don't worry about being perfect—just write what comes to mind every day!

There is hoping your life will improve, and then there is the fire . . . a deep obsession to change and become better, to forge a vibrant and abundant life by sheer will, daily focus, and struggle. The guts to push yourself, lift yourself up, adapt, persist, and be extraordinary. You have the choice every single day: Are you going to go through the motions or are you going to activate what is deep and extraordinary within you?

@BrendonBurchard
#HighPerformanceJournal

Listen to the restlessness. It is telling you to ready yourself, to let loose, to strive for the magic and meaning of life once more.

@BrendonBurchard
#HighPerformanceJournal

Today's Self-Score Category: Health

Score yourself on a scale of 1–10, with 1 being low, on the following general description: I regularly take care of myself so that I can feel my best. I want my overall physical and emotional health (my well-being) to be primed and optimized to make me feel energetic and strong each day. I strive to eat well, sleep well, and work out so that I have the physical vibrancy and stamina to enjoy life and deal with its challenges and opportunities.

1 2 3 4 5 6 7 8 9 10

The challenges I'm facing in this area of my life right now are . . .

The way I would describe my ideal health *at this stage* of my life is . . .

One new action or habit that I could try that would improve this area of my life is . . .

One thing I could stop thinking about, worrying about, focusing on, or doing to improve this area of my life is . . .

What's happening in your life today? What are you thinking about, feeling, or experiencing? How are your health, career, relationships, and mood? What were your intentions for today? What received most of your focus? What decisions did you make? How are things turning out? What emotions came up for you today? What habits made your day better? What strengths did you exhibit today? What tasks or goals did you achieve that you feel good about? What did you learn about someone today? What is something you appreciated today, or are appreciating at this stage of your life? Just start writing now. Don't worry about being perfect—just write what comes to mind every day!

If my future best self (a version of you 10–20 years older, who is even stronger, more capable, and more successful than you had ever imagined yourself to be) showed up on my doorstep today and looked at my current circumstances, these are the actions my future self would tell me to take right away to change my life for the better . . .

[This is a prompt about gaining *clarity* for your future. It's a good habit to ask yourself these types of questions often. What does your future self know you need to change? What do they want you to start thinking about and start doing? What do they want you to stop thinking about and stop doing? What do they hope for you? What wisdom do they deliver to you? Ask yourself: What can I do every single day to get more clarity about my day and life?]

What's happening in your life today? What are you thinking about, feeling, or experiencing? How are your health, career, relationships, and mood? What were your intentions for today? What received most of your focus? What decisions did you make? How are things turning out? What emotions came up for you today? What habits made your day better? What strengths did you exhibit today? What tasks or goals did you achieve that you feel good about? What did you learn about someone today? What is something you appreciated today, or are appreciating at this stage of your life? Just start writing now. Don't worry about being perfect—just write what comes to mind every day!

Listen: Put everything, all of it, all of you, absolutely everything into life. You could just exist and survive, or you can etch a fiery streak of life across the sky, my friend. There is a greater pulse in you, a brilliant charge, and it is readying itself, and it is saying live—live, my friend, engage this moment, come back to life, awaken, rejuvenate, recharge.

@BrendonBurchard
#HighPerformanceJournal

Give yourself some credit. You've got a
big heart, you've made it through this far,
and you are always, always, always
stronger than you think.

@BrendonBurchard
#HighPerformanceJournal

One person whom I need to reach out to, lead, care for, or work hard for on this day is . . .

. . . and what they need from me, and how I can show up well for them is . . .

[What's going on for this person? What do you think they want or need? How can you be of service? What's most important to you in your relationship with this person? What's most important to them?]

What's happening in your life today? What are you thinking about, feeling, or experiencing? How are your health, career, relationships, and mood? What were your intentions for today? What received most of your focus? What decisions did you make? How are things turning out? What emotions came up for you today? What habits made your day better? What strengths did you exhibit today? What tasks or goals did you achieve that you feel good about? What did you learn about someone today? What is something you appreciated today, or are appreciating at this stage of your life? Just start writing now. Don't worry about being perfect—just write what comes to mind every day!

A surprise gift, note, or sign of appreciation I could give to someone I love or care for is . . .

[Who has been deserving or needing some appreciation from you? Why do you feel they need it? Have you neglected them, and if so, how can you re-engage? What's a little surprise that could really make their day?]

What's happening in your life today? What are you thinking about, feeling, or experiencing? How are your health, career, relationships, and mood? What were your intentions for today? What received most of your focus? What decisions did you make? How are things turning out? What emotions came up for you today? What habits made your day better? What strengths did you exhibit today? What tasks or goals did you achieve that you feel good about? What did you learn about someone today? What is something you appreciated today, or are appreciating at this stage of your life? Just start writing now. Don't worry about being perfect—just write what comes to mind every day!

The 3 people I am most grateful for in my life are . . .

[Why are you grateful for each person specifically? What positive things did you learn from them? How are you applying what you learned from them in your life today?]

What's happening in your life today? What are you thinking about, feeling, or experiencing? How are your health, career, relationships, and mood? What were your intentions for today? What received most of your focus? What decisions did you make? How are things turning out? What emotions came up for you today? What habits made your day better? What strengths did you exhibit today? What tasks or goals did you achieve that you feel good about? What did you learn about someone today? What is something you appreciated today, or are appreciating at this stage of your life? Just start writing now. Don't worry about being perfect—just write what comes to mind every day!

Do not fear throwing full energy into life,
to love others with a mad and reckless
enthusiasm, and to pursue interests
and dreams with childish curiosity.

@BrendonBurchard
#HighPerformanceJournal

No great person ever made history without
having guilt thrown at them or suffering some
backlash from those who didn't like or appreciate
their independence, discipline, or single-mindedness.

@BrendonBurchard
#HighPerformanceJournal

Living purposefully, at this stage of my life, means that . . .

[What does it mean to live with purpose this year? What does that mean you value and prioritize? How do you feel when you are on purpose? How can you live more purposefully each day? What should you start doing to feel more purpose, and what should you shed that isn't purposeful?]

What's happening in your life today? What are you thinking about, feeling, or experiencing? How are your health, career, relationships, and mood? What were your intentions for today? What received most of your focus? What decisions did you make? How are things turning out? What emotions came up for you today? What habits made your day better? What strengths did you exhibit today? What tasks or goals did you achieve that you feel good about? What did you learn about someone today? What is something you appreciated today, or are appreciating at this stage of your life? Just start writing now. Don't worry about being perfect—just write what comes to mind every day!

What makes me most confident is . . .

. . . and the way I "turn on" confidence when I need it is . . .

[You've been confident before. What made you feel that way? How can you summon that feeling again? What would you have to say to yourself? What would you have to do? How would you carry yourself, stand, gesture, and speak? What steps can you take to become more confident and demonstrate more confidence?]

What's happening in your life today? What are you thinking about, feeling, or experiencing? How are your health, career, relationships, and mood? What were your intentions for today? What received most of your focus? What decisions did you make? How are things turning out? What emotions came up for you today? What habits made your day better? What strengths did you exhibit today? What tasks or goals did you achieve that you feel good about? What did you learn about someone today? What is something you appreciated today, or are appreciating at this stage of your life? Just start writing now. Don't worry about being perfect—just write what comes to mind every day!

You are beautifully, impossibly unique.
Own that and you can stop apologizing and
minimizing and start living and celebrating.

@BrendonBurchard
#HighPerformanceJournal

Only two things are going to change
your life: Something new comes into
your life, like a new strategy, a new tool,
or a new idea . . . but your life can also
change because something new comes
from within. A new fire, a new commitment,
a new drive, a new belief in yourself and
how much you deserve your dreams.

@BrendonBurchard
#HighPerformanceJournal

Today's Self-Score Category: Mind+Emotion

Score yourself on a scale of 1–10, with 1 being low, on the following general description: I keep a positive outlook and attitude. I'm cultivating a sense of joy and peace in my life so that I can experience positive emotions and relationships. I take care of myself by being mindful to the energy, focus, and emotions I really want to experience and generate in life.

1 2 3 4 5 6 7 8 9 10

The challenges I'm facing in this area of my life right now are . . .

The way I would describe my ideal daily reality in this category *at this stage* of my life is . . .

One new action or habit that I could try that would improve this area of my life is . . .

One thing I could stop thinking about, worrying about, focusing on, or doing to improve this area of my life is . . .

What's happening in your life today? What are you thinking about, feeling, or experiencing? How are your health, career, relationships, and mood? What were your intentions for today? What received most of your focus? What decisions did you make? How are things turning out? What emotions came up for you today? What habits made your day better? What strengths did you exhibit today? What tasks or goals did you achieve that you feel good about? What did you learn about someone today? What is something you appreciated today, or are appreciating at this stage of your life? Just start writing now. Don't worry about being perfect—just write what comes to mind every day!

A few habits that I need to start (or stick to better) in order to have more mental and physical energy every day include . . .

[These are habits of energy. What should you do to rest more, recover better, and feel rejuvenated and energized more often? Where do you feel tired? What's going on there? What can you do to optimize your total health to feel better? What daily practices could keep you happy, peaceful, less stressed, and healthy as you strive for bigger goals?]

What's happening in your life today? What are you thinking about, feeling, or experiencing? How are your health, career, relationships, and mood? What were your intentions for today? What received most of your focus? What decisions did you make? How are things turning out? What emotions came up for you today? What habits made your day better? What strengths did you exhibit today? What tasks or goals did you achieve that you feel good about? What did you learn about someone today? What is something you appreciated today, or are appreciating at this stage of your life? Just start writing now. Don't worry about being perfect—just write what comes to mind every day!

Only through real acts of kindness, courage,
and love can we redeem the world.

@BrendonBurchard
#HighPerformanceJournal

And then one day someone or something becomes more important than your immature concerns and wishes for ease, and you are finally activated to extend yourself, to develop, to serve. It's now necessary to stretch and grow because a greater cause than you demands a greater person than you once were. The calling summons up character. The purpose pulls up new powers and potential.

@BrendonBurchard
#HighPerformanceJournal

An upcoming event or situation that might stress me out if I don't prepare well or remind myself to be intentional and in control of my thoughts and feelings is . . .

[Why do you think that situation will be challenging? What can you do to prepare? What can you say to yourself before and during the situation to stay in command of yourself?]

What's happening in your life today? What are you thinking about, feeling, or experiencing? How are your health, career, relationships, and mood? What were your intentions for today? What received most of your focus? What decisions did you make? How are things turning out? What emotions came up for you today? What habits made your day better? What strengths did you exhibit today? What tasks or goals did you achieve that you feel good about? What did you learn about someone today? What is something you appreciated today, or are appreciating at this stage of your life? Just start writing now. Don't worry about being perfect—just write what comes to mind every day!

An action I could take today to add real value to someone I love, care for, or lead would be . . .

[What's something simple you could do for each person in your life? What's something bigger you could do for those who really need you right now? How do you even define "value" in each of these relationships? What would light someone up with joy?]

What's happening in your life today? What are you thinking about, feeling, or experiencing? How are your health, career, relationships, and mood? What were your intentions for today? What received most of your focus? What decisions did you make? How are things turning out? What emotions came up for you today? What habits made your day better? What strengths did you exhibit today? What tasks or goals did you achieve that you feel good about? What did you learn about someone today? What is something you appreciated today, or are appreciating at this stage of your life? Just start writing now. Don't worry about being perfect—just write what comes to mind every day!

The greatest opportunity in my life right now that I am so grateful for is . . .

[Don't get stuck in thinking about what you have—think about what's possible. Think about all the open doors to learning, the projects available to you, the choices you have, the blessings you've been granted. Just write about what you are (or could be) excited about and why you are grateful!]

What's happening in your life today? What are you thinking about, feeling, or experiencing? How are your health, career, relationships, and mood? What were your intentions for today? What received most of your focus? What decisions did you make? How are things turning out? What emotions came up for you today? What habits made your day better? What strengths did you exhibit today? What tasks or goals did you achieve that you feel good about? What did you learn about someone today? What is something you appreciated today, or are appreciating at this stage of your life? Just start writing now. Don't worry about being perfect—just write what comes to mind every day!

If you've quit on your dream, and your heart still longs for its achievement, only action will remedy the suffering.

@BrendonBurchard
#HighPerformanceJournal

You are not stuck; you are closed, fixated on a certain view of who you are, what's possible, and what rules you must follow. Transformation requires a new level of openness and humility. Only when we are truly open will we activate the curiosity and willingness to try new things. There is no new bold adventure for you without walking through an open gate. Raise your head and lift your eyes, young warrior; there is a greater field of possibility in front of you. Be open to change and miracles and new paths of action, for your destiny is still being written.

@BrendonBurchard
#HighPerformanceJournal

On my final days on this planet, I would love to know that during my lifetime I was always the type of person who . . .

[If you're happy at the end, who did you become? What choices did you consistently make? How did you show up? What makes you proud? At the end, what makes you proud of how you lived—what did you choose to do, to avoid, to care about, to give? How did you show up? How did you love? What mattered to you?]

What's happening in your life today? What are you thinking about, feeling, or experiencing? How are your health, career, relationships, and mood? What were your intentions for today? What received most of your focus? What decisions did you make? How are things turning out? What emotions came up for you today? What habits made your day better? What strengths did you exhibit today? What tasks or goals did you achieve that you feel good about? What did you learn about someone today? What is something you appreciated today, or are appreciating at this stage of your life? Just start writing now. Don't worry about being perfect—just write what comes to mind every day!

If I were going to become even more proud of who I am, and I were going to live more congruently with that vision of myself, I would have to start . . .

[This is a prompt about congruence. It's about living in alignment with the best of who you are. So, what would you have to start doing to live in greater congruence with who you really are, what you really believe, and what you really value and desire in life?]

What's happening in your life today? What are you thinking about, feeling, or experiencing? How are your health, career, relationships, and mood? What were your intentions for today? What received most of your focus? What decisions did you make? How are things turning out? What emotions came up for you today? What habits made your day better? What strengths did you exhibit today? What tasks or goals did you achieve that you feel good about? What did you learn about someone today? What is something you appreciated today, or are appreciating at this stage of your life? Just start writing now. Don't worry about being perfect—just write what comes to mind every day!

No one can quiet you without your permission. And no one can open you up and release your full power but you.

@BrendonBurchard
#HighPerformanceJournal

If you don't feel like you've earned your own self-respect yet, when?
If you don't feel like you can be at peace with life, when?
If you don't feel like you can care for yourself, love yourself,
prioritize yourself, then when? What more do you have to go through?
What more do you have to try? What more do you have to achieve?
If you keep waiting for someday to be at peace with yourself,
then every day between now and then will be an incessant
and unnecessary struggle. You can strive satisfied and with
peace in your heart; it's simply a choice.

@BrendonBurchard
#HighPerformanceJournal

Today's Self-Score Category: Partner/Love

Score yourself on a scale of 1–10, with 1 being low, on the following general description: I feel a consistently deep, trusting, appreciative, soulful, loving connection with my significant other. I am patient, respectful, and attentive to my partner's needs. Alternative if single: I live each day through my heart and demonstrate compassion and love for others.

1 2 3 4 5 6 7 8 9 10

The challenges I'm facing in this area of my life right now are . . .

The way I would describe my ideal daily reality in this category *at this stage* of my life is . . .

One new action or habit that I could try that would improve this area of my life is . . .

One thing I could stop thinking about, worrying about, focusing on, or doing to improve this area of my life is . . .

What's happening in your life today? What are you thinking about, feeling, or experiencing? How are your health, career, relationships, and mood? What were your intentions for today? What received most of your focus? What decisions did you make? How are things turning out? What emotions came up for you today? What habits made your day better? What strengths did you exhibit today? What tasks or goals did you achieve that you feel good about? What did you learn about someone today? What is something you appreciated today, or are appreciating at this stage of your life? Just start writing now. Don't worry about being perfect—just write what comes to mind every day!

The things I've been telling myself that I *should do* have not yet
become *must do's* because . . .

[List all the things you've been saying you want to do. Now go write why
each of those things is necessary—why is it a must that you do them?
How can you raise your psychological necessity and focus in order to get
them done? How can you create deeper motivation or higher stakes so
that you follow through? Who could you tell about what you truly want to
be or achieve in life so that you have some support or accountability?]

What's happening in your life today? What are you thinking about, feeling, or experiencing? How are your health, career, relationships, and mood? What were your intentions for today? What received most of your focus? What decisions did you make? How are things turning out? What emotions came up for you today? What habits made your day better? What strengths did you exhibit today? What tasks or goals did you achieve that you feel good about? What did you learn about someone today? What is something you appreciated today, or are appreciating at this stage of your life? Just start writing now. Don't worry about being perfect—just write what comes to mind every day!

The more you compare yourself, the more you cage yourself. Don't compare yourself to others unless it positively motivates you. But do have the awareness about your own growth and potential. Perhaps the comparisons to make are, "Am I becoming a better person than I was last month? Am I being more present and centered, freer in my expression, kinder, more loving, contributing, and loving with passion and heart again?"

@BrendonBurchard
#HighPerformanceJournal

Sometimes the last mistake and regret leads
to the next miracle and reawakening.

@BrendonBurchard
#HighPerformanceJournal

A family member or teammate who I've noticed is discouraged or dissatisfied lately is . . .

. . . and why I think that is, and what I could do to be of service is . . .

[When did you first notice that something is going on? What do you think they are feeling, exactly? Why do you care about this person? What do you think they need? How can you bring light into their world?]

What's happening in your life today? What are you thinking about, feeling, or experiencing? How are your health, career, relationships, and mood? What were your intentions for today? What received most of your focus? What decisions did you make? How are things turning out? What emotions came up for you today? What habits made your day better? What strengths did you exhibit today? What tasks or goals did you achieve that you feel good about? What did you learn about someone today? What is something you appreciated today, or are appreciating at this stage of your life? Just start writing now. Don't worry about being perfect—just write what comes to mind every day!

I could have made today better for someone I love or care for if I had just done this . . .

[This isn't a guilt party! It's about self-evaluation, not self-judgment—it's being aware of how we show up for others.]

What's happening in your life today? What are you thinking about, feeling, or experiencing? How are your health, career, relationships, and mood? What were your intentions for today? What received most of your focus? What decisions did you make? How are things turning out? What emotions came up for you today? What habits made your day better? What strengths did you exhibit today? What tasks or goals did you achieve that you feel good about? What did you learn about someone today? What is something you appreciated today, or are appreciating at this stage of your life? Just start writing now. Don't worry about being perfect—just write what comes to mind every day!

You made it through another few days. Did you develop more gratitude? Did you notice things you once took for granted and give thanks? Did you realize the hardships of others and send up prayers? Did you recognize struggle and treat others more kindly? Did you choose focus and discipline when distraction could so easily win? Did you take action to protect and build your future or disappear into comforts and drama?

@BrendonBurchard
#HighPerformanceJournal

This is the perfect day to demonstrate gratitude, to call someone and say, "I love you. You've been a positive force in my life."

@BrendonBurchard
#HighPerformanceJournal

The strengths and skills that I've developed over my life that I'm most proud of are . . .

[What are your core strengths? What skills help you succeed? How did you develop each of those strengths and skills specifically? How can you apply those strengths and skills to your current or new opportunities?]

What's happening in your life today? What are you thinking about, feeling, or experiencing? How are your health, career, relationships, and mood? What were your intentions for today? What received most of your focus? What decisions did you make? How are things turning out? What emotions came up for you today? What habits made your day better? What strengths did you exhibit today? What tasks or goals did you achieve that you feel good about? What did you learn about someone today? What is something you appreciated today, or are appreciating at this stage of your life? Just start writing now. Don't worry about being perfect—just write what comes to mind every day!

The achievements that I would be most proud of at the end of my life are . . .

[Think of achievements holistically—mental, emotional, social, physical, financial, relational. What did you give? Where did you go? What did you accomplish in each area of your life that makes you proud?]

What's happening in your life today? What are you thinking about, feeling, or experiencing? How are your health, career, relationships, and mood? What were your intentions for today? What received most of your focus? What decisions did you make? How are things turning out? What emotions came up for you today? What habits made your day better? What strengths did you exhibit today? What tasks or goals did you achieve that you feel good about? What did you learn about someone today? What is something you appreciated today, or are appreciating at this stage of your life? Just start writing now. Don't worry about being perfect—just write what comes to mind every day!

If I were going to become even more energized and healthy so that I had the mental, emotional, and physical energy and stamina I needed to achieve my purpose over the long term, I would have to start . . .

[What habits would you need to begin? What habits would you have to stop doing? What would make you feel energized and alive?]

What's happening in your life today? What are you thinking about, feeling, or experiencing? How are your health, career, relationships, and mood? What were your intentions for today? What received most of your focus? What decisions did you make? How are things turning out? What emotions came up for you today? What habits made your day better? What strengths did you exhibit today? What tasks or goals did you achieve that you feel good about? What did you learn about someone today? What is something you appreciated today, or are appreciating at this stage of your life? Just start writing now. Don't worry about being perfect—just write what comes to mind every day!

When the world questions your abilities, respond
with your actions. Don't justify—demonstrate.

@BrendonBurchard
#HighPerformanceJournal

I feel alive today because today is a blessing.
In this moment, I can find misery or meaning,
boredom or motivation. I can expand the hatred in
the world, or I can amplify love. In all the chaos,
I can find stillness and joy within. All is well,
and nothing has to happen to "give" me more
happiness in life. I simply choose to be happy now,
to be grateful now, to be a source of love and light
for others. I am whole. I am ready. This is my day.

@BrendonBurchard
#HighPerformanceJournal

Today's Self-Score Category: Family

Score yourself on a scale of 1–10, with 1 being low, on the following general description: I am present with my family. I am creating deep connection, fun, and positive energy with the family members that I keep in contact with. It's evident that I love my family and I'm doing my best for them. I try to forgive their mistakes and be compassionate with them.

1 2 3 4 5 6 7 8 9 10

The challenges I'm facing in this area of my life right now are . . .

The way I would describe my ideal daily reality in this category *at this stage* of my life is . . .

One new action or habit that I could try that would improve this area of my life is . . .

One thing I could stop thinking about, worrying about, focusing on, or doing to improve this area of my life is . . .

What's happening in your life today? What are you thinking about, feeling, or experiencing? How are your health, career, relationships, and mood? What were your intentions for today? What received most of your focus? What decisions did you make? How are things turning out? What emotions came up for you today? What habits made your day better? What strengths did you exhibit today? What tasks or goals did you achieve that you feel good about? What did you learn about someone today? What is something you appreciated today, or are appreciating at this stage of your life? Just start writing now. Don't worry about being perfect—just write what comes to mind every day!

The main activities and projects that deserve my greatest focus right now, which will move me faster toward my goals and success, are . . .

[This is a prompt about *productivity*. What 5 steps would get you to where you want to go the most efficiently and effectively? Which projects or activities matter the most? What outputs do you need to create more of? What should you stop doing, quit, or get off your plate? What do you need to remind yourself of every day to be more productive?]

What's happening in your life today? What are you thinking about, feeling, or experiencing? How are your health, career, relationships, and mood? What were your intentions for today? What received most of your focus? What decisions did you make? How are things turning out? What emotions came up for you today? What habits made your day better? What strengths did you exhibit today? What tasks or goals did you achieve that you feel good about? What did you learn about someone today? What is something you appreciated today, or are appreciating at this stage of your life? Just start writing now. Don't worry about being perfect—just write what comes to mind every day!

A few decisions that I could make soon that would demonstrate high standards or moral goodness to the people I love, care for, lead, or serve would include . . .

[What would really show what you value and stand for? What decision would make you proud of yourself? What demonstrates that you walk your talk? What would be an important and inspiring decision here?]

What's happening in your life today? What are you thinking about, feeling, or experiencing? How are your health, career, relationships, and mood? What were your intentions for today? What received most of your focus? What decisions did you make? How are things turning out? What emotions came up for you today? What habits made your day better? What strengths did you exhibit today? What tasks or goals did you achieve that you feel good about? What did you learn about someone today? What is something you appreciated today, or are appreciating at this stage of your life? Just start writing now. Don't worry about being perfect—just write what comes to mind every day!

Once you stop needing and seeking validation
for all the work you've put in, then the work
itself becomes artful, meaningful, fulfilling.

@BrendonBurchard
#HighPerformanceJournal

When someone is rude to you, don't let your ego jump into the fight. You don't need to have the last word or a storybook ending. Walk away, stay centered, love yourself, and don't judge humanity by a few bad apples.

@BrendonBurchard
#HighPerformanceJournal

Something that could have helped me feel more connected to other people lately would have been . . .

[Think broadly here: What do you need from others that would make you feel more connected? What do you think they need from you? What makes a great relationship with others? How can you demonstrate that? Who do you need to request more of that from?]

What's happening in your life today? What are you thinking about, feeling, or experiencing? How are your health, career, relationships, and mood? What were your intentions for today? What received most of your focus? What decisions did you make? How are things turning out? What emotions came up for you today? What habits made your day better? What strengths did you exhibit today? What tasks or goals did you achieve that you feel good about? What did you learn about someone today? What is something you appreciated today, or are appreciating at this stage of your life? Just start writing now. Don't worry about being perfect—just write what comes to mind every day!

The 3 greatest lessons I've learned about myself this year, which I'm grateful for, that really helped me discover or decide something important about myself were . . .

[Don't be afraid to include hard lessons learned from "negative" events too. How did you learn each of those 3 lessons? What new decisions did you make? How are you applying those lessons today? How could 1 of those lessons help you right now in an area you feel stuck in?]

What's happening in your life today? What are you thinking about, feeling, or experiencing? How are your health, career, relationships, and mood? What were your intentions for today? What received most of your focus? What decisions did you make? How are things turning out? What emotions came up for you today? What habits made your day better? What strengths did you exhibit today? What tasks or goals did you achieve that you feel good about? What did you learn about someone today? What is something you appreciated today, or are appreciating at this stage of your life? Just start writing now. Don't worry about being perfect—just write what comes to mind every day!

The goals I would love to achieve by the end of the next 12 months include . . .

[Brainstorm goals in every area of your life: mind, body, spirit, love, family, friends, mission, adventure, experiences, finances, things, learning, skills, etc. Write the goals down and why you want to achieve them. Put some dates next to each one, and at least 1 major step that would be required to achieve it. Don't worry about the perfect answers—just brainstorm!]

What's happening in your life today? What are you thinking about, feeling, or experiencing? How are your health, career, relationships, and mood? What were your intentions for today? What received most of your focus? What decisions did you make? How are things turning out? What emotions came up for you today? What habits made your day better? What strengths did you exhibit today? What tasks or goals did you achieve that you feel good about? What did you learn about someone today? What is something you appreciated today, or are appreciating at this stage of your life? Just start writing now. Don't worry about being perfect—just write what comes to mind every day!

Character isn't developed by trying to become famous or a millionaire . . . character is developed by seeking to become a better human to those you love, interact with, and serve.

@BrendonBurchard
#HighPerformanceJournal

Keeping one's attitude positive, especially
when the world conspires to make us mad,
is one of the great accomplishments of life

@BrendonBurchard
#HighPerformanceJournal

If I were going to have more authentic, intentional, and meaningful relationships with all the people around me, I would have to start . . .

[Think about this both globally and specifically. How would you have to behave in general around other people? Then think of how you'd have to act around specific people in your life—who are they and how can you improve those relationships?]

What's happening in your life today? What are you thinking about, feeling, or experiencing? How are your health, career, relationships, and mood? What were your intentions for today? What received most of your focus? What decisions did you make? How are things turning out? What emotions came up for you today? What habits made your day better? What strengths did you exhibit today? What tasks or goals did you achieve that you feel good about? What did you learn about someone today? What is something you appreciated today, or are appreciating at this stage of your life? Just start writing now. Don't worry about being perfect—just write what comes to mind every day!

Today's Self-Score Category: Friends

Score yourself on a scale of 1–10, with 1 being low, on the following general description: My immediate social circle of friends brings connection, fun, and positive energy into my life. I seek out positive people, and I do my very best to bring positive energy and real authenticity into all my relationships. I spend enough time with friends.

1 2 3 4 5 6 7 8 9 10

The challenges I'm facing in this area of my life right now are . . .

The way I would describe my ideal daily reality in this category *at this stage* of my life is . . .

One new action or habit that I could try that would improve this area of my life is . . .

One thing I could stop thinking about, worrying about, focusing on, or doing to improve this area of my life is . . .

What's happening in your life today? What are you thinking about, feeling, or experiencing? How are your health, career, relationships, and mood? What were your intentions for today? What received most of your focus? What decisions did you make? How are things turning out? What emotions came up for you today? What habits made your day better? What strengths did you exhibit today? What tasks or goals did you achieve that you feel good about? What did you learn about someone today? What is something you appreciated today, or are appreciating at this stage of your life? Just start writing now. Don't worry about being perfect—just write what comes to mind every day!

If I were going to become even more influential with the people I care for the most and those I lead or serve, then I would have to do these things . . .

[Think of the most important people (or groups of people) in your life—write each person's name down or list out the groups (e.g., family, customers, team, etc.). How could you improve that relationship? How would you develop more trust, connection, and influence? Could you be more present for them? Challenge them more? Be a better role model? Add more value? What would it take to deepen your relationship and influence?]

What's happening in your life today? What are you thinking about, feeling, or experiencing? How are your health, career, relationships, and mood? What were your intentions for today? What received most of your focus? What decisions did you make? How are things turning out? What emotions came up for you today? What habits made your day better? What strengths did you exhibit today? What tasks or goals did you achieve that you feel good about? What did you learn about someone today? What is something you appreciated today, or are appreciating at this stage of your life? Just start writing now. Don't worry about being perfect—just write what comes to mind every day!

If the size of your dreams and
ambitions are freaking you out,
then you're on the right path.

@BrendonBurchard
#HighPerformanceJournal

Discipline does not emerge like a sudden burst of energy or emotion. It is summoned from your identity and obsession. You say, "Who the hell am I really, and what matters to me? And if it really matters, then it's my job to light the fire and get at it." Discipline isn't a ready feeling and it doesn't always relate with knowing an exact path; it's pulled from the depths each day and thrust into the world over and over again like a spear of purpose.

@BrendonBurchard
#HighPerformanceJournal

Some major events or projects that are coming up that will require me to be a great leader to those I influence are . . .

[How can you prepare for these events or projects? How can you set people up for success? What will be the major challenges, and how will you overcome them? What will be the values you'll communicate and stand for throughout?]

What's happening in your life today? What are you thinking about, feeling, or experiencing? How are your health, career, relationships, and mood? What were your intentions for today? What received most of your focus? What decisions did you make? How are things turning out? What emotions came up for you today? What habits made your day better? What strengths did you exhibit today? What tasks or goals did you achieve that you feel good about? What did you learn about someone today? What is something you appreciated today, or are appreciating at this stage of your life? Just start writing now. Don't worry about being perfect—just write what comes to mind every day!

The best lessons that I've learned about other people lately are . . .

[What did you learn about someone specifically? How did you learn this about them? Were you surprised to learn this? Where you happy with what you learned? Are you still curious to learn more? How can you apply what you've learned about this person(s) to improve or change your relationship with them?]

What's happening in your life today? What are you thinking about, feeling, or experiencing? How are your health, career, relationships, and mood? What were your intentions for today? What received most of your focus? What decisions did you make? How are things turning out? What emotions came up for you today? What habits made your day better? What strengths did you exhibit today? What tasks or goals did you achieve that you feel good about? What did you learn about someone today? What is something you appreciated today, or are appreciating at this stage of your life? Just start writing now. Don't worry about being perfect—just write what comes to mind every day!

The top 5 values that I hold most dear in my life are . . .

[What is each value, why is it important, and how did you learn it?
How could you apply any of those values to a current challenge or
opportunity you are facing?]

What's happening in your life today? What are you thinking about, feeling, or experiencing? How are your health, career, relationships, and mood? What were your intentions for today? What received most of your focus? What decisions did you make? How are things turning out? What emotions came up for you today? What habits made your day better? What strengths did you exhibit today? What tasks or goals did you achieve that you feel good about? What did you learn about someone today? What is something you appreciated today, or are appreciating at this stage of your life? Just start writing now. Don't worry about being perfect—just write what comes to mind every day!

The goals I would love to achieve by the end of the next
3 years include . . .

[Why do you want each goal? What are the big steps needed to
achieve each goal? What changes do you need to make now in order
to align with those long-term goals? What should you start doing and
stop doing?]

What's happening in your life today? What are you thinking about, feeling, or experiencing? How are your health, career, relationships, and mood? What were your intentions for today? What received most of your focus? What decisions did you make? How are things turning out? What emotions came up for you today? What habits made your day better? What strengths did you exhibit today? What tasks or goals did you achieve that you feel good about? What did you learn about someone today? What is something you appreciated today, or are appreciating at this stage of your life? Just start writing now. Don't worry about being perfect—just write what comes to mind every day!

If I were going to start feeling more cared for and appreciated by those around me, I would have to ask people to . . .

[Think of specific people and write what you want from them. What would you love for them to do in order for you to feel more cared for and appreciated? What can you actually say to them—how can you communicate that request? What should you remember about the person before you talk to them? How can you have a productive conversation? What might make them feel more cared for and appreciated too?]

What's happening in your life today? What are you thinking about, feeling, or experiencing? How are your health, career, relationships, and mood? What were your intentions for today? What received most of your focus? What decisions did you make? How are things turning out? What emotions came up for you today? What habits made your day better? What strengths did you exhibit today? What tasks or goals did you achieve that you feel good about? What did you learn about someone today? What is something you appreciated today, or are appreciating at this stage of your life? Just start writing now. Don't worry about being perfect—just write what comes to mind every day!

Today's Self-Score Category: Mission

Score yourself on a scale of 1–10, with 1 being low, on the following general description: I feel clear, energized, and fulfilled by my work and contributions to the world. I believe my work or day's effort adds real value and is a true reflection of my best efforts and contributions. I am truly engaged and excited by what I'm doing—it feels like a mission, calling, or purpose.

1 2 3 4 5 6 7 8 9 10

The challenges I'm facing in this area of my life right now are . . .

The way I would describe my ideal daily reality in this category *at this stage* of my life is . . .

One new action or habit that I could try that would improve this area of my life is . . .

One thing I could stop thinking about, worrying about, focusing on, or doing to improve this area of my life is . . .

What's happening in your life today? What are you thinking about, feeling, or experiencing? How are your health, career, relationships, and mood? What were your intentions for today? What received most of your focus? What decisions did you make? How are things turning out? What emotions came up for you today? What habits made your day better? What strengths did you exhibit today? What tasks or goals did you achieve that you feel good about? What did you learn about someone today? What is something you appreciated today, or are appreciating at this stage of your life? Just start writing now. Don't worry about being perfect—just write what comes to mind every day!

We think that something magical and uncommon
and mind-blowing must happen to indicate that
we are alive and progressing and lucky. And yet,
right here in the common everyday moment is where
all the universe crackles and ignites and surges in
our soul. The magic is here. Now. In this blessed breath.

@BrendonBurchard
#HighPerformanceJournal

Achievement is not your problem—alignment is.

@BrendonBurchard
#HighPerformanceJournal

One thing I could do today that is a little outside of my comfort zone is to (try, ask for, express, take a big step, etc.) . . .

[What have you been waiting to do but were a little afraid of? What would be a first step? What haven't you asked for? What do you really need or desire? What's a big ambition that you're finally going to go after? What would be something you could do or start that's bold and would truly push you in a new direction?]

What's happening in your life today? What are you thinking about, feeling, or experiencing? How are your health, career, relationships, and mood? What were your intentions for today? What received most of your focus? What decisions did you make? How are things turning out? What emotions came up for you today? What habits made your day better? What strengths did you exhibit today? What tasks or goals did you achieve that you feel good about? What did you learn about someone today? What is something you appreciated today, or are appreciating at this stage of your life? Just start writing now. Don't worry about being perfect—just write what comes to mind every day!

The attitude I'd like the people around me to adopt more of is . . .

. . . and the way that I could lead them to feel and demonstrate that attitude even more is . . .

[What have you been noticing about other people's attitudes? Why do you think this is unsatisfactory or needing change? What do you want for others? How can you be the role model?]

What's happening in your life today? What are you thinking about, feeling, or experiencing? How are your health, career, relationships, and mood? What were your intentions for today? What received most of your focus? What decisions did you make? How are things turning out? What emotions came up for you today? What habits made your day better? What strengths did you exhibit today? What tasks or goals did you achieve that you feel good about? What did you learn about someone today? What is something you appreciated today, or are appreciating at this stage of your life? Just start writing now. Don't worry about being perfect—just write what comes to mind every day!

If I wanted to bring together the positive and supportive people in my life, I could create this event to do it . . .

[Who makes the list? When is the event? What's the goal of bringing them together? How can you make it fun and memorable? What else can you do to deepen your relationships with these people?]

What's happening in your life today? What are you thinking about, feeling, or experiencing? How are your health, career, relationships, and mood? What were your intentions for today? What received most of your focus? What decisions did you make? How are things turning out? What emotions came up for you today? What habits made your day better? What strengths did you exhibit today? What tasks or goals did you achieve that you feel good about? What did you learn about someone today? What is something you appreciated today, or are appreciating at this stage of your life? Just start writing now. Don't worry about being perfect—just write what comes to mind every day!

Everything you have experienced in life has served a purpose:
It brought you here, to this exact point. Your struggles and
tragedies and triumphs brought you here. To this night.
To this moment where you can now choose to be happy,
where you can now choose to serve with excellence, where
you can now open up to love, where you can now live as
your highest self. You've been through enough. Now LIVE.

@BrendonBurchard
#HighPerformanceJournal

When it feels like there is no hope, simplify.

@BrendonBurchard
#HighPerformanceJournal

A big decision that I made or big risk that I took in my life that turned out really well for me was . . .

[What was the context of that decision? What were the results of the decision or action you took? Why are you grateful for how things turned out? What did you learn?]

What's happening in your life today? What are you thinking about, feeling, or experiencing? How are your health, career, relationships, and mood? What were your intentions for today? What received most of your focus? What decisions did you make? How are things turning out? What emotions came up for you today? What habits made your day better? What strengths did you exhibit today? What tasks or goals did you achieve that you feel good about? What did you learn about someone today? What is something you appreciated today, or are appreciating at this stage of your life? Just start writing now. Don't worry about being perfect—just write what comes to mind every day!

The person who I want to grow into and become in my life is the kind of person who . . .

[The kind of person who thinks what? Values what? Treats other people how? Spends their days feeling what emotions? Contributes what? Lives and loves and serves how?]

What's happening in your life today? What are you thinking about, feeling, or experiencing? How are your health, career, relationships, and mood? What were your intentions for today? What received most of your focus? What decisions did you make? How are things turning out? What emotions came up for you today? What habits made your day better? What strengths did you exhibit today? What tasks or goals did you achieve that you feel good about? What did you learn about someone today? What is something you appreciated today, or are appreciating at this stage of your life? Just start writing now. Don't worry about being perfect—just write what comes to mind every day!

If I were going to feel like I was making a real difference each day, these are the things I would want to focus on or do more consistently . . .

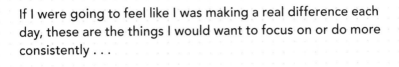

.

[What does *making a difference* mean to you? What would you have to do each day in order to make that difference? What prevents you from doing it? What would help you do it more? What would make you feel most fulfilled in making your difference? How would you know if you've made the difference you want—what would have to happen, what results would you see, what does "success" look like in making your impact?]

What's happening in your life today? What are you thinking about, feeling, or experiencing? How are your health, career, relationships, and mood? What were your intentions for today? What received most of your focus? What decisions did you make? How are things turning out? What emotions came up for you today? What habits made your day better? What strengths did you exhibit today? What tasks or goals did you achieve that you feel good about? What did you learn about someone today? What is something you appreciated today, or are appreciating at this stage of your life? Just start writing now. Don't worry about being perfect—just write what comes to mind every day!

Just because people want to put things
on your plate because you're good
doesn't mean you should let them.

You forgot the magic of now and you're looking for tomorrow to make you happy when it's right here. It's a choice, it's a decision, it's an intention, it's a reconnection with the moment each day. Stop going through the day going through the motions; reconnect with the minute. Take notice of your breath, take notice of what you're paying attention to, appreciate the small things. Be present now because, trust me, if you can't learn to be present now, or you don't feel like life is going great, when it becomes great, you won't notice either

@BrendonBurchard
#HighPerformanceJournal

Today's Self-Score Category: Experiences

Score yourself on a scale of 1–10, with 1 being low, on the following general description: I plan special experiences—trips, adventures, nights out, time to connect or disconnect—so that I enjoy life. I give enough time to the things I love in life, including to my hobbies, interests, and non-work goals and adventures.

1 2 3 4 5 6 7 8 9 10

The challenges I'm facing in this area of my life right now are . . .

The way I would describe my ideal daily reality in this category *at this stage* of my life is . . .

One new action or habit that I could try that would improve this area of my life is . . .

One thing I could stop thinking about, worrying about, focusing on, or doing to improve this area of my life is . . .

What's happening in your life today? What are you thinking about, feeling, or experiencing? How are your health, career, relationships, and mood? What were your intentions for today? What received most of your focus? What decisions did you make? How are things turning out? What emotions came up for you today? What habits made your day better? What strengths did you exhibit today? What tasks or goals did you achieve that you feel good about? What did you learn about someone today? What is something you appreciated today, or are appreciating at this stage of your life? Just start writing now. Don't worry about being perfect—just write what comes to mind every day!

The main struggle I've been facing this last month has been . . .

. . . and if I were advising or mentoring someone dealing with the same struggle, I'd advise them to . . .

[What is the struggle and why do you think it's happening? What emotions does it create for you, and how do you handle them? How have you been dealing with the struggle—facing it, avoiding it, tackling it? What would help you handle it better? What could help you gain more perspective? The next time you feel a negative emotion come up, what can you say to yourself to be strong and optimistic as you deal with this?]

What's happening in your life today? What are you thinking about, feeling, or experiencing? How are your health, career, relationships, and mood? What were your intentions for today? What received most of your focus? What decisions did you make? How are things turning out? What emotions came up for you today? What habits made your day better? What strengths did you exhibit today? What tasks or goals did you achieve that you feel good about? What did you learn about someone today? What is something you appreciated today, or are appreciating at this stage of your life? Just start writing now. Don't worry about being perfect—just write what comes to mind every day!

If I could motivate or push others around me to higher standards of excellence, I would first start with . . .

[How do you role model this? Who needs the help the most? What is that standard you're trying to reach, exactly? What does excellence look like to you? How will you communicate it and enlist others to participate and be the champions of these ideas?]

What's happening in your life today? What are you thinking about, feeling, or experiencing? How are your health, career, relationships, and mood? What were your intentions for today? What received most of your focus? What decisions did you make? How are things turning out? What emotions came up for you today? What habits made your day better? What strengths did you exhibit today? What tasks or goals did you achieve that you feel good about? What did you learn about someone today? What is something you appreciated today, or are appreciating at this stage of your life? Just start writing now. Don't worry about being perfect—just write what comes to mind every day!

If the only challenges you are facing in life right now are the ones life has thrown at you, then you are not directing your own destiny—you are merely reacting to the world. You are not guiding yourself. The greatest challenges we face in life should be the ones we decide to take on to truly feel life and fulfill our potential.

@BrendonBurchard
#HighPerformanceJournal

When people say, "I can't," it's usually code for "I am unwilling to do the long-term training and conditioning necessary to achieve that."

@BrendonBurchard
#HighPerformanceJournal

A stressful event or issue I'm having in my relationship with a loved one is . . .

. . . and some ways that I could handle this issue or improve the relationship include . . .

[Break down the stressful event or issue: What's been happening? How is it making you feel? How could you manage your emotions as it happens or as you deal with it? What is the outcome you're after? What's most important in this relationship?]

What's happening in your life today? What are you thinking about, feeling, or experiencing? How are your health, career, relationships, and mood? What were your intentions for today? What received most of your focus? What decisions did you make? How are things turning out? What emotions came up for you today? What habits made your day better? What strengths did you exhibit today? What tasks or goals did you achieve that you feel good about? What did you learn about someone today? What is something you appreciated today, or are appreciating at this stage of your life? Just start writing now. Don't worry about being perfect—just write what comes to mind every day!

The hardest lesson I ever learned that ended up helping me in
my life was . . .

[How did you learn the lesson? What was happening then—what were
you experiencing at that time in your life? What specifically did you learn,
and how did it change your life? How can you apply that lesson-learned
to the challenges you're facing today?]

What's happening in your life today? What are you thinking about, feeling, or experiencing? How are your health, career, relationships, and mood? What were your intentions for today? What received most of your focus? What decisions did you make? How are things turning out? What emotions came up for you today? What habits made your day better? What strengths did you exhibit today? What tasks or goals did you achieve that you feel good about? What did you learn about someone today? What is something you appreciated today, or are appreciating at this stage of your life? Just start writing now. Don't worry about being perfect—just write what comes to mind every day!

The absolute most important projects that I'm working on this month include . . .

[What are the projects and why are they important to you? What do you need to do to move each project forward? What will it take to complete them? What will you need to learn and do? Who can help you go faster? What projects or distractions should you not focus on? How can you motivate yourself each day to focus on these projects? (Hint: Get the GrowthDay app!)]

What's happening in your life today? What are you thinking about, feeling, or experiencing? How are your health, career, relationships, and mood? What were your intentions for today? What received most of your focus? What decisions did you make? How are things turning out? What emotions came up for you today? What habits made your day better? What strengths did you exhibit today? What tasks or goals did you achieve that you feel good about? What did you learn about someone today? What is something you appreciated today, or are appreciating at this stage of your life? Just start writing now. Don't worry about being perfect—just write what comes to mind every day!

You are capable of remarkable things
that you could never foretell and will
never discover without taking action.

@BrendonBurchard
#HighPerformanceJournal

Believe in your ability to figure things out.
With enough time, effort, and discipline,
you will learn and grow and achieve. You
will bring your art and mission and dreams
to fruition. Trust in yourself.

@BrendonBurchard
#HighPerformanceJournal

If I were going to develop real mastery of specific skills in my life or career, I would have to start learning and mastering these things . . .

[List the skills you want to learn and master on this page. Why do you care about these specific skills? Which do you want to focus on mastering first? How good do you want to get at each skill, and how will you become excellent at it?]

What's happening in your life today? What are you thinking about, feeling, or experiencing? How are your health, career, relationships, and mood? What were your intentions for today? What received most of your focus? What decisions did you make? How are things turning out? What emotions came up for you today? What habits made your day better? What strengths did you exhibit today? What tasks or goals did you achieve that you feel good about? What did you learn about someone today? What is something you appreciated today, or are appreciating at this stage of your life? Just start writing now. Don't worry about being perfect—just write what comes to mind every day!

Today's Self-Score Category: Spirit

Score yourself on a scale of 1–10, with 1 being low, on the following general description: I feel connected to the present moment and vitally alive in my spirit. I am congruent with my beliefs and behaviors, and I keep my faith and values at the forefront of my decisions and daily actions.

1 2 3 4 5 6 7 8 9 10

The challenges I'm facing in this area of my life right now are . . .

The way I would describe my ideal daily reality in this category *at this stage* of my life is . . .

One new action or habit that I could try that would improve this area of my life is . . .

One thing I could stop thinking about, worrying about, focusing on, or doing to improve this area of my life is . . .

What's happening in your life today? What are you thinking about, feeling, or experiencing? How are your health, career, relationships, and mood? What were your intentions for today? What received most of your focus? What decisions did you make? How are things turning out? What emotions came up for you today? What habits made your day better? What strengths did you exhibit today? What tasks or goals did you achieve that you feel good about? What did you learn about someone today? What is something you appreciated today, or are appreciating at this stage of your life? Just start writing now. Don't worry about being perfect—just write what comes to mind every day!

If I were going to become more creative—thinking of new ideas and doing more things that energized my mind and passions—I would have to start . . .

[This is a prompt for creativity. So, what would make you more creative? What would energize your mind, and how can you incorporate that more into your work and everyday life? What would you have to learn? What should you start doing, and what should you stop doing that isn't bringing you great creative energy?]

What's happening in your life today? What are you thinking about, feeling, or experiencing? How are your health, career, relationships, and mood? What were your intentions for today? What received most of your focus? What decisions did you make? How are things turning out? What emotions came up for you today? What habits made your day better? What strengths did you exhibit today? What tasks or goals did you achieve that you feel good about? What did you learn about someone today? What is something you appreciated today, or are appreciating at this stage of your life? Just start writing now. Don't worry about being perfect—just write what comes to mind every day!

The leadership principles that I believe are the most important to be demonstrating to the people I care for and influence right now are . . .

[What principles matter to you, where did they come from, and why do they matter? How can you demonstrate these principles? Who can you share these with? What problem or situation can you or those you lead apply these to? What other principles are going to be important in the next 12 months?]

What's happening in your life today? What are you thinking about, feeling, or experiencing? How are your health, career, relationships, and mood? What were your intentions for today? What received most of your focus? What decisions did you make? How are things turning out? What emotions came up for you today? What habits made your day better? What strengths did you exhibit today? What tasks or goals did you achieve that you feel good about? What did you learn about someone today? What is something you appreciated today, or are appreciating at this stage of your life? Just start writing now. Don't worry about being perfect—just write what comes to mind every day!

You don't need to create a masterpiece
every day; you need to get some
oil on the canvas every day.

@BrendonBurchard
#HighPerformanceJournal

If your guard is up, let it down. If you've constructed a defensive wall to protect yourself and keep all the bad guys out, don't forget who that wall also prevents from getting in: the good guys.

@BrendonBurchard
#HighPerformanceJournal

Something I've said or done to someone I care for recently that I wish I could take back was . . .

[What happened? Why do you think you did what you did? How did the person respond? What do you wish happened? What can you do to repair the relationship, if needed? How can you avoid repeating the same mistake in the future? Who do you really want to be for this person, and how can you demonstrate that?]

What's happening in your life today? What are you thinking about, feeling, or experiencing? How are your health, career, relationships, and mood? What were your intentions for today? What received most of your focus? What decisions did you make? How are things turning out? What emotions came up for you today? What habits made your day better? What strengths did you exhibit today? What tasks or goals did you achieve that you feel good about? What did you learn about someone today? What is something you appreciated today, or are appreciating at this stage of your life? Just start writing now. Don't worry about being perfect—just write what comes to mind every day!

A day in my recent life that just seemed so blessed or
perfect was . . .

[Describe the day and what happened. What was your life like that day?
Why did you appreciate that day so much? Is there anything you did or
learned that day that you could replicate in some way again?]

What's happening in your life today? What are you thinking about, feeling, or experiencing? How are your health, career, relationships, and mood? What were your intentions for today? What received most of your focus? What decisions did you make? How are things turning out? What emotions came up for you today? What habits made your day better? What strengths did you exhibit today? What tasks or goals did you achieve that you feel good about? What did you learn about someone today? What is something you appreciated today, or are appreciating at this stage of your life? Just start writing now. Don't worry about being perfect—just write what comes to mind every day!

If I had to explain to someone I was mentoring what makes me happy and successful—or could make me even more happy and successful—I would say these things . . .

[Write about each one—what makes you happy and what makes you successful. Don't fear bragging here; this is your private journal! Happiness and success are hard won—so how would you advise others to reach for them? What works for you? What doesn't? If you had to write your field manual for becoming happier and more successful, this is the place to write it!]

What's happening in your life today? What are you thinking about, feeling, or experiencing? How are your health, career, relationships, and mood? What were your intentions for today? What received most of your focus? What decisions did you make? How are things turning out? What emotions came up for you today? What habits made your day better? What strengths did you exhibit today? What tasks or goals did you achieve that you feel good about? What did you learn about someone today? What is something you appreciated today, or are appreciating at this stage of your life? Just start writing now. Don't worry about being perfect—just write what comes to mind every day!

Someday, when you least expect it, you will be
called on to serve. Prepare yourself. Develop skill.
Learn. Master your craft. Be ready for that call.

Listening well is about giving up control.
It's releasing your perspective, holding
back your impulse to speak or prove yourself.
It's living in the moment with the person you
are listening to and truly feeling their world.

@BrendonBurchard
#HighPerformanceJournal

If I were going to enjoy my life even more and experience greater presence and depth in my everyday life, I would have to start . . .

[This is about enriching your life more! What will help you become more present? What will make life and your relationships, career, and goals feel more meaningful, deeper?]

What's happening in your life today? What are you thinking about, feeling, or experiencing? How are your health, career, relationships, and mood? What were your intentions for today? What received most of your focus? What decisions did you make? How are things turning out? What emotions came up for you today? What habits made your day better? What strengths did you exhibit today? What tasks or goals did you achieve that you feel good about? What did you learn about someone today? What is something you appreciated today, or are appreciating at this stage of your life? Just start writing now. Don't worry about being perfect—just write what comes to mind every day!

Today's Self-Score Category: Finances

Score yourself on a scale of 1–10, with 1 being low, on the following general description: I am being responsible in how I spend my money. I'm saving money for my future. I'm learning the skills necessary to develop my ability to earn even more. I am happy with my lifestyle and allow myself to enjoy what I've built and earned.

1 2 3 4 5 6 7 8 9 10

The challenges I'm facing in this area of my life right now are . . .

The way I would describe my ideal daily reality in this category *at this stage* of my life is . . .

One new action or habit that I could try that would improve this area of my life is . . .

One thing I could stop thinking about, worrying about, focusing on, or doing to improve this area of my life is . . .

What's happening in your life today? What are you thinking about, feeling, or experiencing? How are your health, career, relationships, and mood? What were your intentions for today? What received most of your focus? What decisions did you make? How are things turning out? What emotions came up for you today? What habits made your day better? What strengths did you exhibit today? What tasks or goals did you achieve that you feel good about? What did you learn about someone today? What is something you appreciated today, or are appreciating at this stage of your life? Just start writing now. Don't worry about being perfect—just write what comes to mind every day!

The subject that I need to study more deeply in order to be more competent, capable, and valued is . . .

[What do you already love to learn that adds value that you can go deeper on? What topics are everyone at work talking about that you need to understand and master? Why is it absolutely necessary for you to improve in these areas? What skills are required for you to go to the next level? What books can you read; what mentors can you seek or follow; what courses can you take? What simple steps or habits can you practice each week to get better?]

What's happening in your life today? What are you thinking about, feeling, or experiencing? How are your health, career, relationships, and mood? What were your intentions for today? What received most of your focus? What decisions did you make? How are things turning out? What emotions came up for you today? What habits made your day better? What strengths did you exhibit today? What tasks or goals did you achieve that you feel good about? What did you learn about someone today? What is something you appreciated today, or are appreciating at this stage of your life? Just start writing now. Don't worry about being perfect—just write what comes to mind every day!

Some areas in my life where I feel overcommitted as a leader are . . .

[Where are you overcommitted, stressed out, or lacking boundaries?
What do you already know needs to be done to handle the situation?]

What's happening in your life today? What are you thinking about, feeling, or experiencing? How are your health, career, relationships, and mood? What were your intentions for today? What received most of your focus? What decisions did you make? How are things turning out? What emotions came up for you today? What habits made your day better? What strengths did you exhibit today? What tasks or goals did you achieve that you feel good about? What did you learn about someone today? What is something you appreciated today, or are appreciating at this stage of your life? Just start writing now. Don't worry about being perfect—just write what comes to mind every day!

If I wanted to add more play and positive emotions into my most important relationship, I could do this by . . .

[Who do you want to have a more playful relationship with? Why do you feel the relationship isn't as playful as you want? What led to its current state? What could you remind yourself to say or do the next few times you're around this person to imbue more play or positivity into the moment?]

What's happening in your life today? What are you thinking about, feeling, or experiencing? How are your health, career, relationships, and mood? What were your intentions for today? What received most of your focus? What decisions did you make? How are things turning out? What emotions came up for you today? What habits made your day better? What strengths did you exhibit today? What tasks or goals did you achieve that you feel good about? What did you learn about someone today? What is something you appreciated today, or are appreciating at this stage of your life? Just start writing now. Don't worry about being perfect—just write what comes to mind every day!

I feel most lucky about these things in my life right now . . .

[What are your current blessings? What do you really appreciate? Who is in your life, and what opportunities are there that seem serendipitous? What makes you most grateful?]

What's happening in your life today? What are you thinking about, feeling, or experiencing? How are your health, career, relationships, and mood? What were your intentions for today? What received most of your focus? What decisions did you make? How are things turning out? What emotions came up for you today? What habits made your day better? What strengths did you exhibit today? What tasks or goals did you achieve that you feel good about? What did you learn about someone today? What is something you appreciated today, or are appreciating at this stage of your life? Just start writing now. Don't worry about being perfect—just write what comes to mind every day!

Everyone fears they are not enough and sees
their life in many ways unfair, difficult,
filled with error and embarrassment. This is
why we must be kind, supportive, praising. The
world needs your light to balance its shadows.

When you get a second chance, honor
that grace by becoming more intentional,
loving, and courageous this time.

@BrendonBurchard
#HighPerformanceJournal

In order to achieve my goals and manifest my ideal life, I'm going to have to show up each day as my best self. When I'm being my best—when I'm on my "A game"—that's when I think, feel, or behave in these ways . . .

[What does *being your best* mean? What are you like then? How can you show up that way even more?]

What's happening in your life today? What are you thinking about, feeling, or experiencing? How are your health, career, relationships, and mood? What were your intentions for today? What received most of your focus? What decisions did you make? How are things turning out? What emotions came up for you today? What habits made your day better? What strengths did you exhibit today? What tasks or goals did you achieve that you feel good about? What did you learn about someone today? What is something you appreciated today, or are appreciating at this stage of your life? Just start writing now. Don't worry about being perfect—just write what comes to mind every day!

If I were going to feel more content and fulfilled in my everyday life, these things would have to change . . .

[Would you have to adjust your mindset? Change your circumstances? Do a different kind of work? Better manage your time or focus? Meditate on your achievements? What else?]

What's happening in your life today? What are you thinking about, feeling, or experiencing? How are your health, career, relationships, and mood? What were your intentions for today? What received most of your focus? What decisions did you make? How are things turning out? What emotions came up for you today? What habits made your day better? What strengths did you exhibit today? What tasks or goals did you achieve that you feel good about? What did you learn about someone today? What is something you appreciated today, or are appreciating at this stage of your life? Just start writing now. Don't worry about being perfect—just write what comes to mind every day!

Today's Self-Score Category: Learning

Score yourself on a scale of 1–10, with 1 being low, on the following general description: I am curious and pay attention to the world around me so that I can learn new things. I ask questions. I seek to discover new things about myself and others. I have created a personalized curriculum for myself so that I can develop the skills needed to succeed.

1 2 3 4 5 6 7 8 9 10

The challenges I'm facing in this area of my life right now are . . .

The way I would describe my ideal daily reality in this category *at this stage* of my life is . . .

One new action or habit that I could try that would improve this area of my life is . . .

One thing I could stop thinking about, worrying about, focusing on, or doing to improve this area of my life is . . .

What's happening in your life today? What are you thinking about, feeling, or experiencing? How are your health, career, relationships, and mood? What were your intentions for today? What received most of your focus? What decisions did you make? How are things turning out? What emotions came up for you today? What habits made your day better? What strengths did you exhibit today? What tasks or goals did you achieve that you feel good about? What did you learn about someone today? What is something you appreciated today, or are appreciating at this stage of your life? Just start writing now. Don't worry about being perfect—just write what comes to mind every day!

If you care for others, your success will be taken care of.

@BrendonBurchard
#HighPerformanceJournal

We think: If I keep working hard, one day I will achieve balance and harmony. But those things are not achieved in work or the outer world. Balance and harmony come from the mind, from conscious thought, from an in-the-Now decision to allow the world as it is and to allow oneself that daring gift of internal peace.

@BrendonBurchard
#HighPerformanceJournal

The things that I need to be even more consistent about in order to be happier and reach higher performance include . . .

[Brainstorm all the areas you are consistent and not consistent in. What matters most on that list? Why do you think you are consistent or not? What can you do to be more consistent? What would change if you were more consistent—what exactly would you achieve and when? What could motivate you to stay the course?]

What's happening in your life today? What are you thinking about, feeling, or experiencing? How are your health, career, relationships, and mood? What were your intentions for today? What received most of your focus? What decisions did you make? How are things turning out? What emotions came up for you today? What habits made your day better? What strengths did you exhibit today? What tasks or goals did you achieve that you feel good about? What did you learn about someone today? What is something you appreciated today, or are appreciating at this stage of your life? Just start writing now. Don't worry about being perfect—just write what comes to mind every day!

A vision I have for my life, team, or organization that I need to enlist more people to join and support is . . .

[Who do you need to get on board with this vision? What are the traits of the people you want on board with you? Why would they join—what values and outcomes will they be attracted to? What can you do to actively recruit people into your mission? How do you want them to think about themselves? How do you want them to think about other people? How do you want them to think about the world at large?]

What's happening in your life today? What are you thinking about, feeling, or experiencing? How are your health, career, relationships, and mood? What were your intentions for today? What received most of your focus? What decisions did you make? How are things turning out? What emotions came up for you today? What habits made your day better? What strengths did you exhibit today? What tasks or goals did you achieve that you feel good about? What did you learn about someone today? What is something you appreciated today, or are appreciating at this stage of your life? Just start writing now. Don't worry about being perfect—just write what comes to mind every day!

If, 10 years from now, the 3 closest people to me in my life were to describe me to other people, I would hope they say things like this about me . . .

[What do you want each of these 3 people to say about you, specifically? Why does that make you feel good and how can you make those descriptions reality? What do you need to change or demonstrate? What do you hope is absolutely true about yourself 10 years from now? What are the values you clearly stand for? What would make you so happy about your life 10 years from now?]

What's happening in your life today? What are you thinking about, feeling, or experiencing? How are your health, career, relationships, and mood? What were your intentions for today? What received most of your focus? What decisions did you make? How are things turning out? What emotions came up for you today? What habits made your day better? What strengths did you exhibit today? What tasks or goals did you achieve that you feel good about? What did you learn about someone today? What is something you appreciated today, or are appreciating at this stage of your life? Just start writing now. Don't worry about being perfect—just write what comes to mind every day!

Don't fear embarrassment; fear living
a constrained and false life. If you are
rejected for being true to yourself, then
you are simply being divinely guided to
move on to another level of community.

@BrendonBurchard
#HighPerformanceJournal

Doubt increases with inaction. Clarity
reveals itself in momentum. Growth comes
from progress. For all these reasons, BEGIN.

@BrendonBurchard
#HighPerformanceJournal

Ready for another journal, or want to give copies to family or friends?

Visit **GrowthDay.com/store** to order more!

GrowthDay.com/store is also the place to pick up these companion works to help you reach your high performance goals:

THE HIGH PERFORMANCE PLANNER
978-1-4019-5723-0

HIGH PERFORMANCE HABITS
978-1-4019-5285-3

The road to self-mastery never ends, and Brendon will be with you every step of the way!